Chris Crutcher

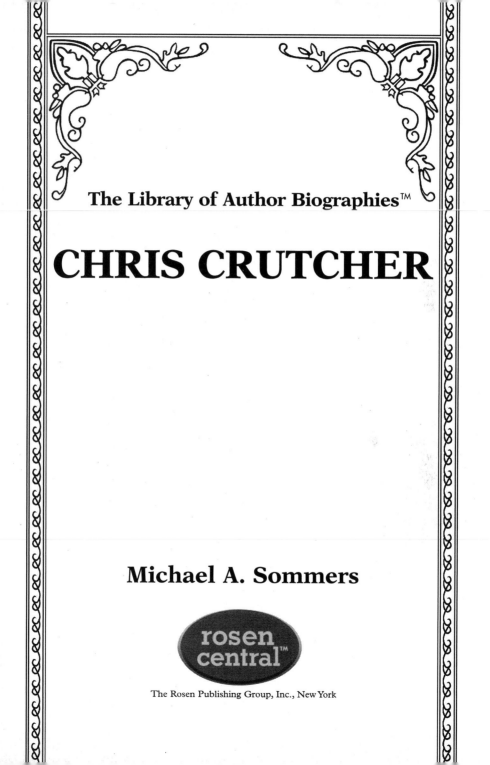

The Library of Author Biographies™

CHRIS CRUTCHER

Michael A. Sommers

rosen central™

The Rosen Publishing Group, Inc., New York

To Annie of Ontario

Published in 2005 by The Rosen Publishing Group, Inc.
29 East 21st Street, New York, NY 10010

Library of Congress Cataloging-in-Publication Data

Sommers, Michael A., 1966-
Chris Crutcher / by Michael A. Sommers.— 1st ed.
    p. cm. — (The Library of author biographies)
Includes bibliographical references and index.
ISBN 1-4042-0325-7 (lib. bdg.)
1. Crutcher, Chris. 2. Authors, American—20th century—Biography.
3. Young adult fiction—Authorship.
I. Title. II. Series.
PS3553.R786Z87 2005
813'.54—dc22

                                                                    2004013100

Manufactured in the United States of America

Blasingame, James. (May 2003). An Interview with Chris Crutcher. *Journal of Adolescent & Adult Literacy*, 46(8), 696-697. Reprinted with permission of James Blasingame and the International Reading Association.
© 1989 *Kirkus Reviews*. Reprinted with permission.
© 2004 *St. Petersburg Times*. Reprinted with permission.
Text from *Presenting Chris Crutcher*, by Terry Davis, 99, Twayne Publishers, © 1997, Twayne Publishers. Reprinted by permission of the Gale Group.
Text from *Something About the Author*, by, 99, Gale Group, © 1999, Gale Group. Reprinted by permission of the Gale Group.
Smith, Louisa. "Limitations on Young Adult Fiction: An Interview with Chris Crutcher." *The Lion and the Unicorn* 16:1 (1992), 66, 67, 69, 71, 72. © The Johns Hopkins University Press. Reprinted with permission of the Johns Hopkins University Press.
Text from the *Horn Book Magazine*, November/December 1987. Reprinted by permission of the Horn Book, Inc., Boston, MA, www.hbook.com.
Text from the *Horn Book Magazine*, September/October 1991. Reprinted by permission of the Horn Book, Inc., Boston, MA, www.hbook.com.
Text from the *Horn Book Magazine*, July/August 1989. Reprinted by permission of the Horn Book, Inc., Boston, MA, www.hbook.com.
Text from *King of the Mild Frontier*. © 2003 by Chris Crutcher. Used with the permission of HarperCollins Children's Books.
Text from *Athletic Shorts: Six Short Stories*. © 1991 by Chris Crutcher. Used with the permission of HarperCollins Children's Books.
Text from *Staying Fat for Sarah Byrnes*. © 1993 by Chris Crutcher. Used with the permission of HarperCollins Children's Books.
Text from *Running Loose*. © 1983 by Chris Crutcher. Used with the permission of HarperCollins Children's Books.
Text from *Chinese Handcuffs*. © 1989 by Chris Crutcher. Used with the permission of HarperCollins Children's Books.
Text from *The Crazy Horse Electric Game*. © 1987 by Chris Crutcher. Used with the permission of HarperCollins Children's Books.

Table of Contents

Introduction: An Unpredictable Life

As predictable as life seems, as many times as I have done things over and over and over, hoping for a different result, it is, in fact, not predictable. In my youth I could never have imagined seeing my name on a book unless I had carved it there with a sharp instrument.[1]

—Chris Crutcher,
King of the Mild Frontier *(2003)*

Such a humorous comment is typical of Chris Crutcher, one of the most popular young adult fiction writers in North America. Crutcher makes this confession on the last page of his recently published autobiography, *King of the Mild Frontier*, in which he recounts important—and often hilarious— episodes from his youth and discusses how they helped shape him as a writer.

Crutcher's amazement at having become a writer in the first place is not so difficult to understand. Growing up in a tiny, northwestern lumber town, Crutcher was much more interested in girls, sports, stealing candy bars from his father's gas station, and rebelling against authority figures than either reading or writing. In fact, he claims he read only one novel during his entire time at high school. And this was because he was going to be tested on it.

Things took a radical turn, however, when Crutcher turned thirty-five. In a matter of months, he sat down and wrote an entire novel from beginning to end. As soon as he finished, he sent the completed manuscript off to an agent, who felt that his book should be published. Soon after, it was.

To this day, Crutcher is almost embarrassed by the surprising ease with which he broke into the growing field of literature for young readers. *Running Loose* (1983) is a story about seventeen-year-old Louie Banks, who seems to have everything going for him: kind, understanding parents, good friends, a wonderful girlfriend, and the respect and popularity afforded by being a starter on the high school football team. But as Crutcher so firmly believes, life is unpredictable. Louie discovers this when he takes a stand and rebels against his football coach, who is willing to do anything to win the season—even resort to violence.

However, standing up for what one believes is right isn't always an easy thing to do. For Louie, it results in the loss of his position on the team as well as his popularity at school. He also loses the respect of many school officials who feel that Louie is a traitor and a coward. When his girlfriend dies in a tragic accident, Louie has to find the strength to deal with his loss and accept that life rarely turns out the way one thinks it will. In doing so, Louie discovers another way of winning—both on and off the field: he becomes a long-distance runner. Through hard work, determination, and a positive attitude, Louie comes to understand that there is always more than one way of living a full life. One simply needs to be open to other possibilities.

Running Loose is a typical Crutcher novel. All of his eight young adult novels, as well as *Athletic Shorts* (1991), his book of short stories for young people, take place in small towns in the Midwest or northwestern United States. They all feature male protagonists on the cusp of adulthood who are suddenly forced to grapple with serious adult issues. Mirroring a young Crutcher, these vividly drawn male characters are angry and impulsive. At the same time, however, they are big-hearted rebels who defy authority. They draw strength from close male buddies and from staunch female friends, some of whom—amid much confusion—become girl-friends. Crutcher's protagonists also draw strength from the discipline, integrity, and purity of sports.

Yes, Crutcher's books are all testosterone-driven stories about football players, iron men, runners, swimmers, wrestlers, and basketball players. Workouts and games are described with dynamic, play-by-play details that are so realistic you can practically smell the sweat. Team loyalty and locker room humor abound. So do the more negative aspects of sports, such as humiliating coaching techniques and the win-at-all-costs mentality and pressures that unfortunately characterize so much of high school athletics. Nonetheless, in Crutcher's world, sports are much more than the thrill of a win or the crush of a loss. They are a metaphor for life, for the struggle to do one's best—not only physically but mentally and spiritually as well. As Crutcher confesses in the foreword to *Athletic Shorts*:

> I like it when my stories are seen by my critics from the same perspective as that in which most human beings are seen by their critics— for doing their best in tough situations, for failure, for excesses, for heart, for the glorious and the ghastly.[2]

Crutcher's protagonists not only struggle on the field or court but off them as well. And unlike sports, where rules are clear, life's rules prove to be much more complex. A longtime child and family therapist, Crutcher knows firsthand about many of the more brutal aspects of some of life's struggles. With directness and honesty, he inserts these serious problems into his fiction—some critics say to an extreme extent. Physical and sexual abuse, discrimination, abortion, drug abuse, suicide, and death are just a few of the more pressing issues that frequently crop up in Crutcher's work.

For young readers, many of whom have similar problems, Crutcher's novels are fitted with characters and situations with which they can identify. Treating his readers as equals, the author provides no easy solutions and no false, neatly wrapped-up endings. Instead, he offers frank and open discussion and options for the resolution—many of them positive—of some of life's most complicated problems.

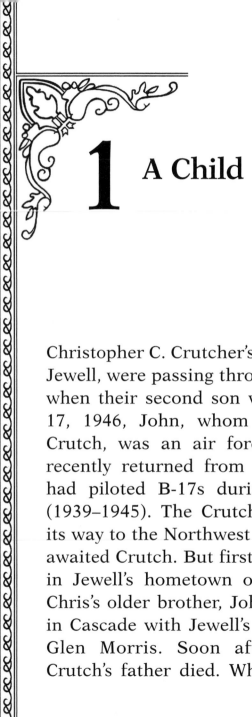

1 A Child

Christopher C. Crutcher's parents, John and Jewell, were passing through Dayton, Ohio, when their second son was born. On July 17, 1946, John, whom everybody called Crutch, was an air force pilot who had recently returned from Europe where he had piloted B-17s during World War II (1939–1945). The Crutcher family was on its way to the Northwest where a flying job awaited Crutch. But first, they made a stop in Jewell's hometown of Cascade, Idaho. Chris's older brother, John Jr., was staying in Cascade with Jewell's parents, May and Glen Morris. Soon after their arrival, Crutch's father died. While he was taking care of his mother, the flying job Crutch had been promised was given to somebody else.

Cascade, Idaho

Without work and with a family to feed, Crutch decided to settle down in Cascade. Glen Morris owned a Mobile Gas service station, and he invited Crutch to work with him. Cascade was a tiny lumber and logging town located in the Rocky Mountains in western-central Idaho. There was only one paved road in town, and the closest movie theater was 80 miles (129 kilometers) away. Most of Cascade's 900 residents were rugged types who liked hunting and the outdoors. When the Crutchers arrived, they moved into a small house across the dirt road from May and Glen Morris's house. This was the house in which Chris grew up.

As a young boy, Chris was close to his grandfather. Glen Morris was a very affectionate man. Having grown up an orphan, sleeping in neighbor's sheds and working at difficult jobs for his food, Glen was sensitive to others' suffering. He was always willing to lend a hand— even to total strangers. Everyone in Cascade knew that if you got stuck in the snow in the middle of the night, you could call Glen Morris to come pull your car out.

"Bawlbaby"

Growing up, Chris was also very close to his parents. They influenced him in many positive ways. As he would later recall in an interview:

> My mother gave me a sense of passion . . . of going with my feelings. And my dad was the balance point to that. He was a tremendously rational [levelheaded] man, the problem solver. He gave me an ability to make things simple . . . and get to what the problem really is.[1]

Later on in life, when Chris became a therapist, he claims that his father's sensible advice helped him much more than any psychology class ever did.

When Crutcher published his first novel, *Running Loose*, he not only dedicated it to Crutch and Jewell but based the kind and perceptive parents of Louie Banks (the seventeen-year-old protagonist) on them. Like Brenda Banks, Jewell was emotional and "good for helping you realize that how you feel is how you feel."[2] Similar to Norm Banks, Crutch owned a gas station and was chairman of the school committee. He believed it was important for people—particularly young people—to think for themselves, even if this meant questioning authority.

Running Loose offers a portrait of life that is very similar to Crutcher's own. The setting of Trout, Idaho, is a faithful replica of Cascade. And like Louie Banks, young Chris worked after school at his dad's gas station. He worked there from the age of nine (with a starting wage of 25¢ an hour) right up until his junior year of college. Aside from filling gas tanks, serving customers, and eavesdropping on the fascinating tales told by older teenage employees, young Chris enjoyed ripping off chocolate bars from the candy machine (at the age of twelve, he had been overjoyed to discover where his father hid the key).

As a boy, Chris tended to take after Jewell. He was highly emotional and fairly impulsive. He had a fierce temper that was quick to flare up when he didn't get what he wanted. When physical or emotional pain overwhelmed him, Chris reacted in one of two ways. He either became violent or he humiliated himself by becoming (as he humorously refers to himself in his autobiography), a big, fat "bawlbaby." As he admits, "The moment I considered myself either the cause or the focus of disappointment, my eyes would squint, my lips would spread wide open over my buck teeth, and it was a race to my chin between tears and snot."[3]

Boys and Men with Tempers

In *King of the Mild Frontier*, Crutcher refers to a story about his temper that his mother loved to tell at bridge games and Christmas get-togethers with her friends.

> Chris was very difficult to deal with, even at an early age. When things didn't go his way, he would throw himself into the air, kick his legs out from under him, and land hard on the floor. I was afraid he'd hurt himself, so I called Dr. Patterson for advice. Dr. Patterson said, "Just roll one of those wooden alphabet blocks under him when he goes up. That should take care of it." So the next time he launched himself, I rolled the block under him and sure enough he never did it again.[4]

As Crutcher is quick to point out in *King of the Mild Frontier*, his mother's tale isn't quite accurate. Although he stopped throwing himself on the floor, he did continue dealing with his frustration, shame, and anger in other destructive ways. Even well into Crutcher's thirties, the roof of his Volkswagen Beetle was constantly damaged because he would punch it from the inside whenever the motor died on a busy street.

These violent ways of dealing with anger and shame later became a constant theme in Crutcher's novels. Like young Chris himself, the teenage males in his books deal with feelings of insecurity and pain by lashing out at others because they are afraid or unable to tell the truth about their circumstances and seek help. In *Running Loose*, Boomer Cowan beats up Louie Banks because his father beats him up. In *Ironman* (1995), in order to stay in school, Bo Brewster (the main protagonist) must enroll in an anger management class because he can't control his pent-up rage toward his father. And in *Whale Talk* (2001), former football hero Rich Marshall deals with his faded glory by abusing his new wife and the young daughter she had with an ex-boyfriend.

Overcoming these feelings and being able to control such outbursts is a result of many factors. As Crutcher knows, it helps to have family you can count on, who can help set you straight. And the luckiest of his protagonists, such as Louie Banks, Eric "Moby" Calhoune (*Staying Fat for Sarah Byrnes*, [1993]) or the Tao "T. J."

Jones (the hero of *Whale Talk*), have parents who trust their kids and stand by them through thick and thin.

More likely, however, parents themselves are the source of their children's pain. This pain can be physical, such as the beatings seventeen-year-old Nortie receives from his father (*Stotan!* [1986]) and Virgil Byrnes's vicious shoving of his daughter, Sarah, against a hot stove (*Staying Fat for Sarah Byrnes*). Yet it can also be emotional—and even unintentional. In *Ironman*, for example, Bo's father punishes him for giving $100 he earned to a homeless man. He did this believing that it was for Bo's own good: his son needed to learn the value of money.

Time and time again, Crutcher returns to the theme of young adults learning to cope with their parents' baggage. It is a situation he can identify with. As a boy, he felt responsible for taking care of his alcoholic mother, who had nobody else to whom she could pour out her troubles. Since Chris's father and his older brother, John, were more emotionally distant, young Chris took it upon himself to try to make his mother feel better. The fact that he never quite succeeded left him feeling frustrated. While Cascade's citizens viewed his parents as a happily married couple,

Chris was forced to confront the less than pretty truth of a sad, alcoholic mother and a distant, unemotional father who refused to acknowledge that there were problems. It wasn't until years later—in his life and in his writing—that Chris Crutcher would begin the difficult task of tackling the sometimes ugly truths in people's lives.

2 A Student

Chris's older brother, John, was a bright student who put a lot of pressure on himself to succeed. According to Chris, he never got a mark lower than an A minus. Witnessing firsthand what it was like to be an academic whiz made young Chris certain that he wanted to live up to his middle initial and be a C student. He certainly didn't want the stress of having to excel at school.

Living Up to His Middle Initial

While his parents and brother loved to read, Chris avoided books like the plague. The only book he claims to have read in high school was Harper Lee's *To Kill a Mockingbird* (1960). The novel had been assigned for a test, and at first, Chris hoped that reading the back cover would be enough to get by. However, the first page sucked him into the story and he ended up reading right through until the end (although he didn't reach the final page until three weeks after the test).

He disliked writing just as much as reading. Instead of concentrating on his homework, in order to keep up his C average (his parents wouldn't have accepted anything less), Chris hit upon a better solution. Over the years, John had filed away all of his homework assignments in a bedroom closet. With the utmost care, Chris would browse through the old reports and assignments and then set to work copying them. He slyly threw in enough spelling mistakes and factual errors to prevent his teachers from becoming suspicious.

Meanwhile, in the classroom, instead of impressing teachers and classmates with his academic talents, Chris attracted attention by being the class clown and rebel. As he admits in an interview, "I didn't want to do anything anybody told me to do."[1]

Rebel with a Cause

Chris's first writing efforts were 500-word essays that teachers assigned him as punishments for misbehaving. The themes usually had to do with the wrongs he had committed. Chris would get very creative with these assignments. Interestingly, in eighth grade, his journalism teacher was so impressed by one of these punishment essays that he persuaded Chris to write for the school newspaper.

Chris took him up on the offer. The column he wrote was called "Chris' Crumbs." Just like *Crispy Pork Rinds*, the underground school paper that Moby and Sarah Byrnes wrote and published in *Staying Fat for Sarah Byrnes*, Chris's columns were smart-mouthed jibes at students and teachers. And like Moby and Sarah Byrnes, Chris enjoyed writing whatever he wanted. In fact, he continued to write the column until his last year of high school.

Other punishments that he received at school were less constructive. Chris remembers the first male teacher he ever had in sixth grade. Mr. Tarter, a local reverend, was a firm believer in punishing kids for sins both real and imagined. If he caught students chewing gum or passing notes, he would send them to the front of the classroom where they would hold their arms straight out at 90-degree angles until they broke into tears. If the offense was really serious, he would place heavy books upon their arms.

Another humiliating situation occurred when Chris was in grade five. It was right before Christmas, and his teacher had asked the class to write down all the words they could find using the letters from "Merry Christmas." The first word Chris marked down was his own name, "Chris." The second was "Christ." When his teacher passed by and glanced at his paper, she immediately demanded that Chris reverse the order of the words. When he refused, thus questioning her authority, she scolded him in front of the class. She said that by writing his name before Christ's, he was committing the Christian sin of pride. Chris was so marked by this event that forty-five years later, he worked it into his novel *Whale Talk*.

Challenging Authority

Moments such as these only increased Chris's sense of frustration and injustice with respect to authority figures—both academic and religious. As an adult writer, he has continually dealt with these themes in his novels. Reflecting his own life, his novels are peopled with teachers, principals, and coaches who are often narrow-minded or bullies (or both).

Instead of trying to earn their students' respect and admiration, they attempt to control them by filling them with fear. As many teens know (and as Crutcher himself discovered the hard way) there is nothing a young person hates and fears more than being humiliated in front of his or her peers. And when religion is used as a tool of instilling fear (by making someone feel evil or sinful), Crutcher can become very critical of religion.

Crutcher takes on religious authority in many of his novels. In *Staying Fat for Sarah Byrnes*, the protagonist, Moby, is enrolled in a course called Contemporary American Thought along with Mark Brittain, a fundamentalist Christian. Backed by Vice Principal Mautz, Mark tries to shut down the class, claiming that the viewpoints expressed (such as those supporting abortion, for example) are blasphemous. During one class, Mark makes the mistake of saying that God is responsible for everything that goes on in the world—both good and bad. For this reason, we shouldn't question the things that happen to us because even the most horrible occurrences (such as

Sarah Byrnes being burnt by her father) are God's will.

Fortunately, Moby's best friend, Steve Ellerby, also takes Contemporary American Thought. The son of an Episcopalian minister, Steve drives around town in a Pontiac station wagon he calls the Christian Cruiser. Meanwhile, Ellerby is still a religious guy who participates in weekly services at his father's church. However, having lived through the pain of having lost his older brother, he doesn't believe God is responsible for everythingin life, not even his brother's death. When he tells the class how he responded to a priest who tried to soothe his pain by assuring him that God works in "strange and mysterious ways," Ellerby's voice echoes Crutcher's. "I figure if those things were in God's jurisdiction [domain], he'd do something different about them. But they aren't. Those are in our jurisdiction."[2]

This view of the world is present in all of Crutcher's novels. From childhood on, Crutcher came to believe that things occur because of people, not because of God. According to Crutcher, neither human beings, nor God, can change bad things that happen. But we can learn how to react to them in a positive way.

The Fairer Sex

Although he had a younger sister named Candy, it was at school that young Chris began what would become a long, complicated (and sometimes humorous) series of relationships with girls. Crutcher himself admits, "Pretty girls were my downfall from way before I had hormones enough to govern my embarrassing behavior."[3] As an adolescent, he went to great lengths to attract the attention of pretty young women. Unfortunately, these attempts often backfired.

Over the years, Chris had failed to impress several girls with his helpfulness and good looks. Because of this, he decided on a new tactic: making a girl laugh. It was with this goal in mind that he nurtured a massive two-inch scab that formed on his arm after he wiped out during track practice. After two months, he carefully peeled the hairy red scab from his arm and packed it in cotton. Then he brought it to school and deposited it on the desk of the much-desired Bonnie Heavrin. Needless to say, the reaction wasn't quite what Chris had anticipated. Bonnie screeched and called him a pig. Furthermore, his English teacher almost kicked him out of class for the rest of the semester.

Courting Paula Whitson

One of the biggest crushes Chris ever had was on a girl named Paula Whitson. In fact, Chris had been silently pining for her ever since first grade. However, in high school, he began courting Paula "like a kid setting fire to an ant with a magnifying glass."[4] He began finding things on the floor—such as pens, notebooks, or money—and giving them to her with the excuse that he thought she had dropped them. Knowing that Paula's parents took after-dinner drives, and they often passed the Crutcher house, Chris took to doing push-ups and sit-ups on the front lawn. He hoped that if Paula was in the car, she would catch sight of his growing muscles.

After years of such courtship rituals, Chris finally worked up the courage to ask Paula to the annual Christmas dance. Although he was thrilled when she accepted, his joy turned to terror as, over the next few weeks, he felt an enormous pimple beginning to grow beneath the surface of his forehead. By the time the dance rolled around, the zit was large enough "to have its own spread in *National Geographic*."[5] Desperate to get rid of it, Chris followed a friend's advice and resorted to the "Coke bottle treatment." He held the mouth of a Coke bottle (which had been dipped in boiling water) around the zit. As the air in the bottle cooled and compressed, the core of the pimple was supposed to be sucked into the bottle. Instead, Chris's attempts resulted in the bottle sticking to his forehead. When he finally got it off, the bottle had left a big, purplish, target-shaped bruise in the middle of his forehead, with the zit as the bull's-eye. It was the last time Paula ever went out with Chris.

Trouble Between the Sexes

Although such romantic encounters are described humorously, they also reveal the difficulty boys (and men) have in communicating with girls (and women). In all of Crutcher's novels, male protagonists and their friends are involved in realistic romantic (often sexual) relationships with females. Just as in real life, in these novels, the relationships between young men and young women are complicated affairs full of conflict and misunderstandings. And just like in life, sometimes love doesn't triumph.

The novel *Chinese Handcuffs* (1989) provides a good example of how difficult male-female relationships can be. Dillon Hemingway, the book's main character, begins the novel by confessing that he has always been in love with Stacey. In turn, Stacey loved Dillon's drug addict brother, Preston, who committed suicide. Later, Dillon begins to fall in love with a basketball star named Jennifer. However, as he learns more about Jennifer and her painful secrets, he realizes that he might never be able to have a romantic relationship with her. He discovers that it will take an incredible amount of therapy for Jennifer to get past the trauma caused by years of sexual abuse at the hands of her father and stepfather.

Weak Boys and Tough Girls

Interestingly, all of Crutcher's male protagonists reveal moments of vulnerability, insecurity, and even cowardice. In contrast, Crutcher's supporting cast of females are tougher, stronger (often physically as well as emotionally), more mature, and brainier than their male counterparts. In *Stotan!*, for example, narrator Walker Dupree spends the entire book vowing to break up with his sweet and sexy girlfriend, Devnee, whom he no longer loves. Instead, he secretly pines for his close friend Elaine, who is having an affair with a teaching assistant. However, he never does work up the courage to be honest and tell Devnee that he doesn't want to be with her anymore. Nor does he have the guts to open up to Elaine. In *The Crazy Horse Electric Game* (1987), jock hero Willie Weaver is on top of the world until a freak accident leaves him disabled. His insecurity, bitterness, and jealousy cause him to lash out at his girlfriend, Jenny. This eventually drives her into the arms of another guy.

In *Presenting Chris Crutcher* (1997), Crutcher's friend and biographer Terry Davis explains the reasons for some men's behavior around women: "Probably the toughest place [for men] to stand up for ourselves, to say who we are and that's the way it is, is in the war zone of romance . . . A lot of men would rather take a beating than tell the truth to a woman, because, as Crutcher says, to tell the truth is to say who we are."[6]

Crutcher himself admits that relationships have always been complicated for him. For this reason, he has never married and doubts he ever will. He has never even lived with a woman, although he has been involved in long-term romantic relationships. As he notes,

> People always say, 'Why is the love stuff always so tentative in your stories?' And the answer is: Because it was always so tentative in my life . . . There was always something to feel bad about. There was always something to be ashamed of . . . There was always a place where you hadn't told the truth because you didn't want to hurt somebody's feelings, or you . . . didn't want to face the way you looked if you told the truth.[7]

3 An Athlete

Sports play such a major role in all of Chris Crutcher's fiction that the jacket covers of his novels feature images of adolescents in the throes of some athletic activity. Inside the books themselves, Crutcher's male protagonists passionately train for and compete in at least one sport. The determination, suspense, and fast-paced action that accompany sports fuel much of the novels' plots and themes. Crutcher's young characters define themselves and each other by their athletic drive, talent, and attitudes toward winning and losing. Meanwhile, parents, particularly fathers, get incredibly wrapped up in their children's athletic performances as do teachers and coaches.

Bellmont Middle School LMC

Unsurprisingly, in Crutcher's hometown of Cascade (and the small midwestern and northwestern towns inhabited by his main characters), high school sports, especially football, were the town's main form of entertainment. Crutcher recalls that, when he was younger, the whole town would shut down during the football games.

The Sporting Life

All of this would lead one to suppose that as a boy, Crutcher himself was a big-time athlete. However, that wasn't at all the case. Unlike his older brother, John, a 6-foot-tall, 230-pound (1.8-meter, 104.3-kilogram) football star, Chris began his first year of high school as a 123-pound (55.8 kg) beanpole "with all the muscle definition of a chalk outline."[1] He could barely do one push-up. And he claims that he could have his hair cut in less time than it took him to run a 100-yard dash. However, with a high school population of fewer than 100 students, Chris, like the other young men, had to be a jock. If not, there wouldn't be enough players to make up a team. Crutcher recalls, "If you didn't show up for football practice on the first day of school, they simply came and got you."[2] It didn't matter whether or not you were a good athlete.

Crutcher claims that his characters are much better athletes than he ever was. Unlike Hawk (*The Crazy Horse Electric Game*), Jennifer (*Chinese Handcuffs*), and T. J. Jones (*Whale Talk*), Crutcher spent most of his high school basketball season on the bench (although, as an adult he improved a lot and he still loves a good pick-up game). Unlike Bo Brewster (*Ironman*) and Louie Banks (*Running Loose*), Crutcher was nothing special at track and field. In fact, Crutcher claims that he never received official times for the first 3-mile (4.82 km) runs in which he competed, because by the time he reached the finish line, "the timers [had] packed up their stop watches and headed for their cars."[3] And at football, he was probably not unlike Louie Banks, who describes himself as "never . . . all that good. Not too big, not too fast, and a lot more desire to be a football player than to play football."[4]

However, what Crutcher did come to enjoy about sports was the deep sense of accomplishment and camaraderie they provided him with. As he would later say, "Finding out how far you can push yourself if you have the support of your friends—that's very important to me about sports."[5] Indeed, in all of Crutcher's novels, athletics is more than just an opportunity for young men to test their stamina, strength, and endurance. It is a way to learn about good sportsmanship and teamwork. Furthermore, the strong male bonds of loyalty and friendship that are forged—not only during games but also during grueling practices, intimate locker-room sessions, and long road trips to faraway games—are a source of pleasure and comfort in a confusing teenage world.

By the time Chris finished high school, he was 6 feet (1.8 m) tall and his once skinny physique was more solid and muscular. He graduated in 1964. On a last minute whim (because he liked the colors of the college catalog), he applied to Eastern Washington State College in Cheney, Washington. Later, he was accepted.

At Eastern, the swimming team was short of swimmers. One day, a member of the team caught sight of Chris doing laps in the college pool and immediately recruited him. Back in Idaho, Chris had swum competitively at school. In fact, he had joined when he discovered that his longtime crush, Paula Whitson, was on the team. But he was about as good at swimming as he was at basketball. However, with a lot of training and some coaching,

Crutcher discovered at Eastern that swimming was his sport.

A Stotan

During his second year in college, he and his teammates were at swim practice when they noticed a sign asking for volunteers for "Stotan Week." Curious, they approached their coach, a tougher-than-nails guy who ran practices like torture sessions and showed he meant business by dressing in his black belt karate gear and using a megaphone.

Stotan Week turned out to be an incredibly intense week of workouts that pushed Crutcher and his teammates to their physical and mental limits. Aside from swimming hundreds of laps, highlights included dozens of push-ups and crab-walking around the pool, out into the snow, and back. During Stotan Week, Crutcher and his teammates all moved in to the dumpy apartment of a swimmer who lived on his own in downtown Cheney. Not only did the experience teach them about their possibilities as athletes, but it also created a lasting bond.

Stotan itself is a combination of two words ("stoic" and "Spartan,"), which together mean "a tough guy that shows no pain."[6] The term was invented by Australian track coach Percy Cerruty to describe famed long-distance runner Herb Elliott, a world record-holder in the 1950s and 1960s. Cerruty claimed that Elliott was the toughest runner he had ever coached. After leaving his Australian teammates in the dust, he would rip off his clothes and go running into the wilderness until he could run no farther. Crutcher's swim coach adapted the concept from land to water and Crutcher himself transformed his Stotan experience to the one shared by Walker, Nortie, Lion, and Jeff in his second novel, *Stotan!* In fact, the Stotan ethic and mentality is celebrated in all of Crutcher's subsequent novels. It is especially present in *Whale Talk*, *Staying Fat for Sarah Byrnes*, and *Ironman* (in which original Stotan, Lion Serbouseck, reappears as a gay teacher who inducts hero Bo Brewster into "Stotanism"), whose protagonists are all competitive swimmers.

Although all the athletes in Crutcher's novels train long and hard, winning is never the primary motive of athletic competition for either the author or his characters. Those who do enter sports with a win-at-all-costs attitude are portrayed in a negative light. Crutcher criticizes players who treat their teammates and opponents with aggression or disdain as well as coaches and parents who believe winning a game (or a season) takes priority over all other aspects of academic and personal life.

Winning Isn't Everything

One of the most dramatic examples of such an attitude is based on an actual event that happened to Crutcher in his first year on the Eastern swim team. While he was in the locker room, he overheard members of the basketball team discuss a private meeting they had just had with their coach. The team was on a winning streak, and it was facing an opposing team whose star player was black. After confessing to his players that he had experienced playing against "them," the coach warned his players that he wanted the black player out of the game by halftime. Players were to use any method possible—including violence—to accomplish this.

Crutcher remembers being shocked that none of the players spoke out against this coach (and his deep shame that he himself remained silent out of embarrassment and fear of getting beat up). Worse was the fact that the players obeyed the coach and injured the black player so badly, he had to leave the game. Eastern's team ended up winning the season, and its coach and players were treated as heroes.

Crutcher was so disgusted by this incident that fifteen years later, he turned the episode into the central conflict of his first novel, *Running Loose*. Only unlike Crutcher, hero Louie Banks *does* have the guts to speak up and defy his racist football coach. Although Louie is kicked off the team and viewed as a hothead and quitter by the school principal, the coach, and much of the school, like all of Crutcher's heroes, Louie is not your stereotypically dumb jock. He is a sensitive, thoughtful athlete who is prepared to defy authority when he feels that those in command are being unjust.

Ultimately, Crutcher likes sports because he views them as one of the few areas in life in which the rules are clear and easy to follow— quite unlike life itself. He believes that being part of a sports team can offer a positive refuge and sense of stability to young people with difficult, chaotic lives. However, at the same time, he never thinks that all rules should be blindly followed, without thinking. Like his characters,

Crutcher considers himself to be an unconventional athlete who is usually quick to rebel against injustice in often conservative sporting circles. In high school, he remembers shocking his principal when he asked why there were no sports teams for girls (the principal's reply was that girls weren't emotionally equipped to play competitive sports). And in college, he publicly supported black runners Tommie Smith and John Carlos when they raised their fists in pride upon winning medals at the 1968 Olympic Games. His attitude earned him a lot of hate mail.

Crutcher's rebellious stance is taken up by complex protagonists such as Bo Brewster (*Ironman*), a star athlete who quits the football team when his coach uses personal humiliation as a training tactic. Similarly, *Chinese Handcuffs*'s Dillon Hemingway, the best male athlete at his high school, frustrates much of the staff when he refuses to play team sports. The vice principal (a former coach) goes so far as to accuse Dillon of being selfish and unpatriotic. Ultimately, Dillon saves his talents for training for the Ironman triathlon. He also manages the girls' basketball team because, as Dillon admits, the coach "knows what athletics is about better than anyone in the business. Her teams win and lose with grace and dignity, and her players never walk away empty-handed, never walk away without a lesson."[7] Dillon's observation echoes Crutcher's own view of athletics. Ultimately, the role of sports is to train young people to be talented players in the game of life.

4 A Teacher

In college, as well as taking sports more seriously, Crutcher also spent much more effort on his academic studies. He took a particular interest in sociology and psychology. Sociology courses gave him a behind-the-scenes look at the role of many institutions, such as schools and churches. In his psychology courses, he learned a lot about how humans beings behave and why. Many of the ideas he studied challenged the notions he had been taught at school and at home.

The Graduate

In his final year of college, Crutcher still hadn't chosen a major. When a school official called him to ask what he was majoring in, Crutcher had no idea what to reply. When he realized most of the courses he had taken were in psychology and sociology, he decided to major in both subjects. When he graduated in 1968, he received a bachelor's degree in sociology-psychology.

After graduation, Crutcher didn't know what to do with his life. Along with a buddy from high school, he climbed into a car and took off across the country. Every time they reached a major highway intersection, they flipped a coin in order to choose which route to take. This method led them as far as Texas, where they got jobs pouring concrete for $2.17 an hour. When they had saved enough money, they spent it all on a trip to Hawaii. When Crutcher returned to the continental United States, he was suntanned and broke. Deciding it might be time to think about a career, he returned to Eastern, where he spent a year earning a teaching certificate. He thought that teaching would provide him with a moneymaking skill.

However, even with his certificate, Crutcher didn't feel ready to teach. Instead, he spent half a year working as a maintenance man at a ski resort in Mount Hood, Oregon. Ultimately, hard manual labor at $2 an hour made him change his mind. When he heard about a teaching job in Kennewick, Washington, he applied and was hired. Known as a "drop-out school," the new school was for students who had quit or been kicked out of public high schools.

Because the school had such a small budget, Crutcher worked as both administrator and teacher. He had to make up the program as he went along. All his efforts revolved around persuading the students to stay enrolled long enough to earn a high school diploma. During his three years at Kennewick, Crutcher learned a lot about what worked with kids and what didn't. He discovered that the key to dealing with his students was to be flexible. If one approach didn't work, it was best to admit failure and try something else.

"The Toughest Place I'd Ever Been"

In 1973, after two years, funding for the school dried up. As a result, Crutcher was forced to look for a new job. He found one teaching social studies at another public high school in Kennewick. However, it wasn't long before he began to feel that working at a regular school was boring. The following year, he moved to California and got a job at another alternative school that turned out to be, as he would later say, the toughest place he'd ever been. This school was in Oakland, a poor city with a high crime rate. Oakland is located across the bay from San Francisco. Lakeside School taught kids of all ages who had been expelled from their regular public schools. Violence, drugs, and alcohol were common. So was not showing up for class. After three years of teaching, Crutcher was so frustrated that he went to speak to the school's director. The director responded to Crutcher's concerns by offering him the job of director. He took it, even though it meant working fifteen-hour days with no pay increase.

His years as a class rebel helped him with teaching and also with making up and enforcing rules at school. At Lakeside, one of the toughest challenges Crutcher faced was dealing with the many kids who acted up because they wanted to get thrown out of school. Crutcher decided that a student could get sent home—especially if he or she were hurting someone else—but that the student could never get expelled. This decision surprised many students, but ultimately, it created a place where everyone had to confront his or her problems and learn how to work and get along together. Crutcher admits that, overall, the school's approach was a success. A lot of the students overcame difficult personal circumstances and earned their diplomas.

Crutcher's experience at the school inspired much of his third novel, *The Crazy Horse Electric Game*. Set in a small town in Montana, the main character, seventeen-year-old Willie Weaver, is a baseball star with everything going for him. Then a waterskiing accident leaves him crippled and slightly brain damaged. After he angrily pushes away his friends and family, loses his girlfriend and his self-esteem, he runs away to Oakland. Saved from a gang of Asian hoodlums, Willie ends up living and working for his rescuer, a bus driver and sometimes criminal. At the same time, he attends Crutcher's fictionalized version of Lakeside, the OMLC (One More Last Chance) School. Run by an unconventional, wise, and exceedingly Crutcher-like director named Andre, its student body is made up of kids whom Andre describes as "pretty damaged."[1]

Willie is damaged, too, but if he is going to grow up, he has to deal with his accident and its consequences. Like all of Crutcher's protagonists, instead of asking "why me?" he must accept responsibility for what happened to him and work on moving forward. In Willie's case, he ignored common rules of safety: he was skiing too fast and wearing a lifejacket that was too big. Although it takes some time, Willie ends up making friends and getting much more of an education than he had expected. With help from Andre, a PE teacher and physical therapist named Lisa, and a diverse collection of courageous new friends (all with their own problems), he learns to accept his disability and to turn it into a capability.

Heroes

In Crutcher's view, this is what being a hero is all about—not pitching a perfect ballgame, but having the guts to overcome life's many obstacles, including one's own damaged self. In the role of teacher/novelist, it is a lesson that he states over and over again. For example, in *Staying Fat for Sarah Byrnes*, Sarah Byrnes is heroic because she stands up to her father and overcomes the effects of the disfiguring scars (both physical and emotional) that he has caused her to have. In *Whale Talk*, the members of the swim team train and compete despite individual handicaps such as brain damage, obesity, and an artificial leg. Although they don't win any championships, they prove that they are just as valuable as other athletes at their school.

Willie Weaver is admirable not only because he earns a high school degree and learns how to play a mean game of basketball but because he acquires the strength to return home to Montana and face the friends and family he walked out on. He needs this strength to deal with the fact that his parents have divorced, his father is a nasty alcoholic, and his former girlfriend hates him. Although some reviewers of *The Crazy Horse Electric Game* criticized Crutcher for this depressing ending, others argued that it merely reflects life itself.

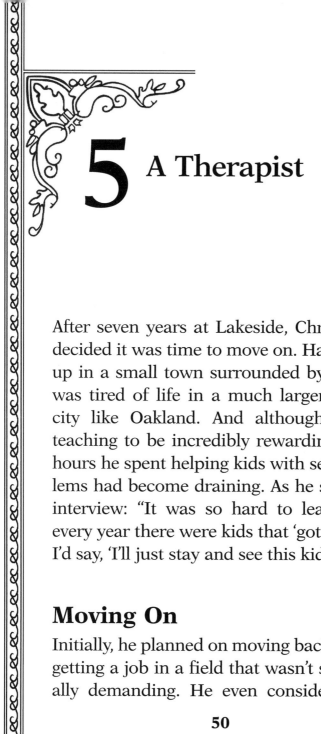

5 A Therapist

After seven years at Lakeside, Chris Crutcher decided it was time to move on. Having grown up in a small town surrounded by nature, he was tired of life in a much larger, sprawling city like Oakland. And although he found teaching to be incredibly rewarding, the long hours he spent helping kids with serious problems had become draining. As he stated in an interview: "It was so hard to leave because every year there were kids that 'got' to me, and I'd say, 'I'll just stay and see this kid through.'"[1]

Moving On

Initially, he planned on moving back north and getting a job in a field that wasn't so emotionally demanding. He even considered selling athletic shoes or working in a spa. Funnily enough, after he had been in Spokane, Washington, for no more than a few months, he took a job coordinating the Spokane Child Protection Team. This was a group that worked with some of the city's toughest child abuse cases. A year later, he also began working as a child and family therapist at the city's Mental Health Center.

As a therapist, many of the kids Crutcher saw were sent to him from Spokane's schools. These were kids with problems so serious that school guidance counselors couldn't help them. As a therapist, Crutcher tried to offer these kids a safe place where they could talk about their feelings, doubts, and fears. Many of them had no other safe place where they could talk and nobody else with whom they could talk. As Crutcher once admitted in an interview: "To me, therapy is allowing kids to come in, close the door, and talk about what life's really like for them."[2]

Therapy Sessions

In his autobiography, Crutcher confesses that of all the complaints he has about his years growing up, the biggest is about the many well-meaning adults—his parents, relatives, and teachers—who lied to him. They told him things that many people want to believe are true about life, such as "love conquers all," "justice always wins the day," or "bad things only happen to bad people."

As an adult, Crutcher understands that these lies were told in order to protect him or prevent him from being disappointed. However, he claims that the disappointment that hit him when he discovered that life really wasn't anything like what the adults had told him was much worse. As many of the protagonists of his novels are forced to discover, life is very unpredictable. If you live according to expectations of how it's supposed to be, you won't survive. However, those who have the courage to face the truth of how life really works, and to meet its many challenges head-on, have a good chance.

Around the same time that Crutcher became a therapist, he wrote and published his first book. He was thirty-five years old. Perhaps it was hardly surprising that the two events coincided. The people, stories, and problems he confronted as a therapist inspired the novels he would write.

As a writer, Crutcher has tackled many issues, most of which are extremely painful and some of which are social taboos. They range from abortion, prostitution, physical and mental handicaps, racism, sexism, and homophobia to alcoholism, AIDS, drug abuse, rape, child abuse, suicide, and death (from illnesses, accidents, and even murder). The detailed exploration of such issues is what makes Crutcher's novels so intensely realistic and compelling to young readers. In a sense, the novels are therapeutic. They invite readers into a private and protective space where they can interact with characters whose problems they might share or identify with.

In fact, in Crutcher's work, readers witness many situations—a pep talk, a workout, a classroom discussion—that are conducted like informal therapy sessions. For example, in both *Stotan!* and *Whale Talk*, the long overnight bus trips to out-of-town swim meets allow characters to let down their guard and share their problems in the presence of coaches and teachers. The same results are achieved at school during the discussions that occur in Mrs. Lemry's Contemporary American Thought class (*Staying Fat for Sarah Byrnes*) and in Mr. Nakatani's anger management group (*Ironman*). By following these in-depth exchanges between young people and adults, readers are able to confront complicated issues with honesty. They are often exposed to realistic viewpoints that they might not always receive from the adults in their lives.

It is for this reason that Crutcher fills his novels with teenagers and adults who display a wide range of complex problems, outlooks, and personalities. In Crutcher's stories, for example, readers meet every kind of parent, teacher, coach, and administrator imaginable: from terrifying child abusers, fragile victims, and strict bullies to wise, supportive, and independent-thinking men and women who are capable of great insight and generosity.

Crutcher once met Robert Cormier, the award-winning author of *The Chocolate War* (1974), when both were participating in a National Council of Teachers of English (NCTE) panel discussion. Cormier, who had just written his young adult novel *Fade* (1988), had read Crutcher's novel *Chinese Handcuffs* and was surprised that Crutcher "used adult wisdom"[3] in his books. Crutcher responded that he likes to use adult characters in his novels because they are able to make sense of things for young protagonists in need of guidance.

Characters such as Dakota and Norm (Louis Banks's boss and dad in *Running Loose*), Max (the swim coach in *Stotan!*), Coach Kathy Sherman (*Chinese Handcuffs*), and Mr. Simet (the English teacher/swim coach in *Whale Talk*) are all adults who go out of their way to help and support students who are in trouble. However, help never means solving the problems for the protagonists. Instead, these adults recognize that teens must make their own decisions about their lives. Crutcher says this was how his father would help him solve problems. He would tease him him with information and ask him questions until young Chris came up with his own solutions.

Truth Telling

Frequently in his books, there is a distinctly Crutcher-like adult character—a teacher, coach, or, more often than not, an actual therapist—whose voice sounds not unlike that of the author himself. Through these characters, Crutcher can let loose some of his own perspectives, which are based on years of considerable experience.

One example of such a character is a therapist named Cyril Wheat, whom Willie Weaver goes to see after his crippling injury in *The Crazy Horse Electric Game*. As Terry Davis points out in *Presenting Chris Crutcher*, Wheat is "a Crutcher persona more Crutcher-like than most, particularly in his sense of humor and his commitment to honesty."[4] According to Davis, the T-shirt Wheat wears, stamped with "Gay Vegetarian Nazis for Jesus," is a direct reference to Crutcher's offbeat humor and clothing. In real life, Crutcher wears a "Nuke the Children" shirt. And the advice Wheat gives Willie reflects the value Crutcher places on honesty. When Willie expresses concern for letting his friends and family know how scared and insecure he is, Wheat has the following to say to him: "A lot of what happens now depends on truth. When you're afraid your girlfriend is going away or your friends are keeping you around just because they feel sorry for you, you have to say that to them."[5]

The importance of the truth is one of the major themes in all of Crutcher's novels and short stories. As a therapist, Crutcher believes that no matter how much it hurts, knowing the truth is the only way that people can heal their pain. When confronted with life's obstacles, Crutcher feels that the best thing a person can do is find the courage to stand up for what he or she believes in.

Perhaps unsurprisingly, Crutcher's willing- ness to fill his fiction with so many true-to-life situations (many of which depict some of the uglier realities of life) has made some adults uneasy. For instance, almost all of Crutcher's novels feature the tragic death of a major character as well as some form of violent physical abuse. Some teachers, parents, and critics of children's literature have objected to the large doses of loss and pain that are present in Crutcher's stories. They worry that these issues are too much for young people to be confronted with.

The response to *Chinese Handcuffs*, for example, was very mixed. The novel features a divorce, a teenage pregnancy, and a teeth-clenching scene in which a cat is tortured to death. The main protagonist, Dillon Hemingway, must deal with his brother's suicide (a crippled drug addict, Preston shoots himself in front of his brother). Dillon must also cope with the knowledge that his girlfriend, Jennifer, is being sexually molested and terrorized by her seemingly perfect stepfather, while her mother does nothing.

Some critics praised the novel. Writing in the *Horn Book* magazine, reviewer Margaret A. Bush noted that Crutcher "constructs his tangled web with intelligent insight, creating a painful, powerful story . . . [that] is [a] compelling, well-paced, and even humorous one of human failing, survival, and hope."[6] However, other reviewers didn't like the novel at all.

The American Library Association (ALA) even refused to review it in its magazine, *Booklist*. Reviewer Stephanie Zvirin later explained why. She said it was "an unsuccessful book—and a disappointment—because the overloaded plot strains the novel's structure."[7] *Kirkus Reviews* echoed this sentiment when a reviewer noted that teenage characters "have been knocked around in Crutcher's other stories, but . . . Crutcher probes so many tender areas here that readers may end by feeling exhausted and emotionally bruised."[8]

Crutcher's reaction is that all of his novels are based on true stories told to him by the patients he sees in therapy. In fact, he often tones down the disturbing tales he is told in his office. He also points out that in real life, "bad times are magnetic to other bad times. And they do pile up on people."[9] However, what matters most to Crutcher is the reaction of the young people for whom he writes his novels. He admits that the critical reaction to *Chinese Handcuffs* originally upset him. But after giving a presentation at a Houston, Texas, high school, a girl came up to Crutcher and said, "I just want you to know that I read *Chinese Handcuffs* and I thought you knew me."[10] It was then that Crutcher realized that the novel was a success with the readers he cared about most.

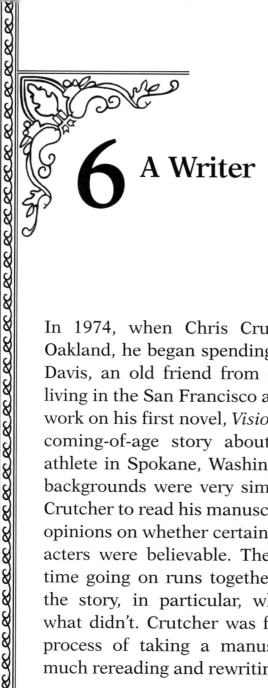

6 A Writer

In 1974, when Chris Crutcher moved to Oakland, he began spending time with Terry Davis, an old friend from college who was living in the San Francisco area. Davis was at work on his first novel, *Vision Quest* (1979), a coming-of-age story about a high school athlete in Spokane, Washington. Since their backgrounds were very similar, Davis asked Crutcher to read his manuscript and give him opinions on whether certain events and characters were believable. They spent a lot of time going on runs together and discussing the story, in particular, what worked and what didn't. Crutcher was fascinated by the process of taking a manuscript and, with much rereading and rewriting, turning it into a complete, polished novel. He was also impressed that his friend could write so well. He started mulling over story ideas of his own. Crutcher recalls: "Here's a guy that I could beat one-on-one in basketball. He wasn't from outer space—he was one guy who rolled up his sleeves and did his storytelling, and I realized that writing was a human thing to do."[1]

The First Novel

Crutcher had never imagined that a regular guy like himself could become a writer—particularly a guy who had never liked reading very much. But Crutcher had always liked listening to stories, and his experiences as an educator and a therapist had turned him into a good listener and observer of human behavior. He also gradually realized that he needed a creative outlet from dealing with the daily crises of people's lives.

Then, in 1980, he found himself with four months of freedom between leaving Lakeside and beginning his job with the Child Protection Team in Spokane. Not knowing what to do with his spare time, he dared himself to write a book. Filled with ideas and unable to forget the impact *To Kill a Mockingbird* had left upon him in high school, Crutcher sat down and, over the next few months, furiously wrote a novel—by hand.

Upon finishing the first draft, he reread the story. Although it was his first writing effort, the novel felt surprisingly complete to him. It didn't even seem to require any rewrites. Eager for another opinion, Crutcher sent a copy to Terry Davis, who had actually been encouraging him to write for years. As soon as he finished reading it, Davis called Crutcher up (at 2 AM) to tell him he loved the novel. He also insisted that Crutcher immediately send it to Davis's agent. Filled with excitement, Crutcher stuffed his manuscript into an envelope, pulled a very long T-shirt over his underwear, and tore off on his motorcycle to the nearest mailbox.

However, when he woke up the next morning, he was immediately struck with fear and doubts. Pouring over his copy of the manuscript, he found numerous grammatical errors and typing mistakes. Some episodes seemed completely wrong. Suddenly, his entire novel seemed like the biggest disaster ever written. Luckily, soon after Crutcher was reassured when he received a phone call from Davis's agent, Liz Darhansoff. She had loved the book and wanted to represent it (pitch the novel to editors in the aim of getting it published). Soon after, Crutcher's first novel, *Running Loose*, was sold to Greenwillow Books in New York. Crutcher was thrilled when, one day in 1983, he opened his mailbox and found himself face to face with a copy of his first published book.

What to Write About—and How

Interestingly, when Crutcher was writing *Running Loose*, he never considered the fact that it would be published as a young adult (YA) novel. In fact, Crutcher didn't even know that there was such a thing as YA fiction. To this day, he has trouble with the term. Ultimately, Crutcher feels that he is a storyteller whose stories appeal to human beings who want to connect with a good story. These readers could be middle school kids, teenagers of the same age of his protagonists (sixteen to eighteen), or adults. In fact, on many occasions, adults have approached him in public to say they love his novels. They also complain about the fact that they never would have read Crutcher if they hadn't known a teen who recommended one of his books to them. Crutcher himself doesn't understand why all of his fiction is only found in the YA sections of bookstores and libraries. He claims that aside from a suspenseful plot and adult protagonists, his one so-called adult novel, *The Deep End* (1992), is no different from his other YA novels.

The fact that Crutcher's fiction is about young people and is largely sold to and read by them has created some problems over the years. Interestingly, however, the problems are not with young readers. They tend to react with great enthusiasm to Crutcher's intensely realistic explorations of their lives. Instead, Crutcher often finds his books attacked by adults—parents, school administrators, and even some teachers and reviewers. Over the years, they have criticized, censored, and even banned Crutcher's books.

In fact, two of Crutcher's novels made *USA Today*'s list of Top Ten Banned Authors (a fact he has no trouble with since other members of the list include Mark Twain, author of the American classics *The Adventures of Tom Sawyer* [1876] and *The Adventures of Huckleberry Finn* [1885] and Kurt Vonnegut, author of important American novels such as *Slaughterhouse-Five* [1969] and *Breakfast of Champions* [1973]). The two books in question were *Athletic Shorts* and *Running Loose*.

A Banned Author

There were two things in particular that caused *Running Loose* to be banned from some school libraries in the United States. The first was an episode that Crutcher himself remembers over-hearing when he was nine years old and was working at his father's gas station. In this scenario, an older high school boy was bragging to his buddies about a good-looking girl he had asked on a date to the movies. According to what young Chris remembers from listening to the story, at the movie theater, the boy offered the girl some pop-corn from the bag on his lap. Reaching her hand into the popcorn, she not only grabbed a handful of crunchy kernels but her date's "thing"[2] as well (he had ripped a hole in the bottom of the bag).

In *Running Loose*, Crutcher has the bully, Boomer Cowans, tell this story in order to reveal his character—that of a crude and lying braggart. The fact that narrator Louie Banks finds the story disgusting hints that Crutcher himself doesn't like such behavior, although he admits it exists. How-ever, many adult critics were horrified to find this sexually explicit episode in a book and they considered it to be vulgar, rude, and unnecessary.

Language Problems

The second problem that Crutcher had to deal with was his use of realistic language. Crutcher had grown up surrounded by locker-room banter at school and the racy stories told by young male garage mechanics at his father's gas station. Before sitting down to write *Running Loose*, he had spent ten years in a tough inner-city public school. For Crutcher, it was natural that the language that made its way into his first and subsequent novels was the often not-so-pretty language used by the young males with whom he came into contact.

Crutcher claims that the original *Running Loose* manuscript was 300 pages long. His editor told him that Greenwillow would publish the book as it was. However, she warned Crutcher that he had used two specific and potentially problematic words so often that it might affect sales, given that many librarians and teachers would refuse to buy the book. After Crutcher removed the two offensive words, he joked that *Running Loose* was close to 200 pages in length. However, for the sake of realism, Crutcher did leave in some instances of swearing.

Most critics praised *Running Loose*. Writing for *Voice of Youth Advocates* (VOYA), Mary K. Chelton said that "first novelists this good"[3] are extremely rare. Zena Sutherland—an influential literary critic, champion of children's literature, and the distinguished editor of the important journal the *Bulletin of the Center for Children's Books*—echoed that view. She declared *Running Loose* to be "an unusually fine first novel."[4] She singled out Crutcher's powerful characterization and the convincing nature of his protagonist's relationships. Writing for *School Library Journal*, Trev Jones was less positive. While she praised this "fine young adult book" for "rais[ing] important issues for adolescents to consider," she referred to "the language, which is peppered throughout with obscenities" as "problematic."[5]

Crutcher's experience with the criticism of *Running Loose* forced him to make some tough decisions. He had to carefully consider whether he would continue to write about the real-life situations and people he knew, hence using the language they actually spoke. Even though he was aware that this would get him into trouble with censors and book banners throughout the United States, he decided that he would not stop writing the way he wanted to. And for over twenty years, in eight novels (including one for adults), a book of short stories, and his recently published autobiography, Crutcher has stayed true to himself, his characters, and his readers.

Staying True

This decision has meant that he can't let critics and censors influence him. Crutcher says, "I was already struggling with an idea some adults had about young adult literature: that its purpose should be to set examples rather than to reflect the truth as the author sees it."[6] Crutcher believed—and still does—that the most important aspect of his writing is communicating the truth about life, even if it means tackling ugly situations and using unpleasant language. He feels strongly that this is what he must do in order to build a bridge between his characters and the young people who read his books. And over the years, as Crutcher continues to work with kids in therapy, he has continued to write about these tough realities.

In November 1998, Crutcher received the Intellectual Freedom Award from the National Council of Teachers of English for his tremendous efforts in defending young adult literature against censorship challenges. As Crutcher says,

> My mission is to write truths as I see them, reflect the world as it appears to me, rather than as others would have it. There are significant amounts of people who think kids should not be exposed in print to what they are exposed to in their lives.[7]

If adults are sometimes divided over so much realism, Crutcher's young readers overwhelmingly appreciate being treated with respect by an author who offers them situations and characters that seem to mirror their own lives. In a study entitled "Chris Crutcher—Hero or Villain? Responses of Parents, Students, Critics, Teachers," writer Betty Greenway points out that Crutcher was one of the most popular guest authors ever at the 1993 Youngstown State University's English Festival, in Rhode Island. At the festival, over 3,000 young people gathered to discuss all forms of young adult fiction. Aside from his ability to portray intense realism, she adds that perhaps part of what draws young readers to novelists such as Crutcher is the fact that adults are offended by some of the contents.

Crutcher's most recent novel, *Whale Talk*, illustrates Greenway's observation. While parents and teachers across the country fought to ban the book because of the language that comes out of the mouth of a five-year-old black girl, kids wrote letters of support to Crutcher in which they praised the novel as being inspirational. Of course, what makes the often brutal episodes of a Crutcher novel bearable, and the novels themselves so entertaining, is the abundant humor that counterbalances the most tragic events. From raunchy jock talk and gross-out bathroom humor to subtle wordplay, irony, and sarcasm, Crutcher's novels contain passages that make teens, and even adults, laugh out loud. While in real life, Crutcher has a reputation for being a very funny man, humor is also something he takes very seriously. As he stated in a recent interview:

> Humor is an amazing healer. I tried to quit the job as chairman of the child protection team for a long time and they'd never let me leave it because they liked my dark humor. They knew we needed it to give perspective, and to be able to laugh while we were doing heartbreaking work.[8]

Writing Professionally

As a youth, Chris Crutcher adopted a rebellious anti-intellectual stance, thinking it was cool to read and write as little as possible. As an adult, however, (although still a rebel) he has become a writer who loves both reading and composing stories. In an interview with Terry Davis, Crutcher compares his writing process to that of a carpenter. Writing a story is like building a structure. However, instead of using wood,

Crutcher uses words. And like carpentry, each word is carefully selected to fit as precisely as possible into the body of the story. Although sometimes it is hard work, this task of choosing the right word (sometimes with the help of a thesaurus) is a lot of fun for Crutcher.

The final product rarely disappoints either readers or reviewers. Over the years, reviewers have, overall, been quick to praise Crutcher's fiction. Although some have criticized his plots, calling them contrived, false, or cluttered, most have hailed his "truly believable male adolescent characters,"[9] his "quick and scorching"[10] dialogue, and his writing style, which "moves like a skilled swimmer—direct, strong, and even."[11] All of Crutcher's novels have been selected as ALA (American Library Association) Best Books for Young Adults. In 1993, he received the ALAN Award for Significant Contribution to Adolescent Literature, and in 2000, he was honored with the prestigious Margaret A. Edwards Award for his entire body of work.

While Crutcher has become one of North America's most popular young adult authors, he hasn't changed very much. Now in his late fifties, he continues to be an enthusiastic runner, swimmer, and basketball player. He loves to crack

The Writing Process

Crutcher usually begins a story with a certain real-life character or situation in mind. However, as he types ideas into his laptop computer, the real-life inspiration quickly takes on a life of its own, moving in sometimes surprisingly new directions. Often, this starting-off phase can be the most difficult for Crutcher; he likens it to pulling teeth. He'd rather do anything else—from watching TV to washing dishes—than face a blank computer screen. Going for a run helps a lot. Although, over the years, he has spent many Sunday nights trying to plan what he'll write during the coming week, he has yet to stick to any fixed writing schedule. In general, he writes whenever he feels the urge and has the time. Once he gets into the middle—or heart—of the story, Crutcher writes quite quickly for as long as he can. For this reason, he likes laptops, which he can carry around everywhere he goes.

When writing, Crutcher doesn't let himself think about his audience. He says imagining how a book will be read or received makes him self-conscious, which tends to stop him from thinking or writing spontaneously. He prefers to let his editor worry about the audience and what is appropriate or not. However, he usually has a clear idea of the age of his male protagonists; they are almost always between sixteen and eighteen years old. Crutcher chooses this age group because he feels that late adolescence is, as he says, often "the first time young people see that they have some influence over their world . . . [and are] on the edge of having to live their lives themselves."[12]

While he is actually writing, Crutcher requires quiet surroundings, but when he begins editing, he often listens to country or classic rock 'n' roll music. Editing is something Crutcher is very disciplined about. He likes the idea of fine-tuning and fixing a passage until he thinks it works. In fact, he considers himself better as an editor than as a writer. To see how a section of a work-in-progress advances, he sometimes reads portions to the young readers he visits in schools and libraries around the United States.

jokes, especially ones that poke fun at himself. An eternal rebel, he continues to speak out against injustice and protest against authority figures—be they book censors, right-wing religious figures, or narrow-minded bullies.

Since 1995, he has become a full-time writer, yet he continues to work part-time as a child and family therapist in Spokane. His success as a writer means he doesn't have to charge his clients. In fact, he claims he was never comfortable receiving payment for guidance and information that should be everybody's birthright. Best of all, says Crutcher, being a writer keeps him "in touch with the truth about being alive on planet Earth," He continues, "it keeps me humble. And it gives me sources for stories."[13]

Interview with Chris Crutcher

James Blasingame recently exchanged e-mails with Chris Crutcher about Crutcher's new autobiography, *King of the Mild Frontier*.

Blasingame: Your brother John seems to have been like most big brothers in that he tempted you into acting in ways that were not in your best interest but often in his. How does he feel about being revealed these many years later?

Crutcher: Needless to say we don't see those events through the exact same colored lens. I recently spoke at his retirement party (he was wrapping about thirty-five years as an accountant) and I read the "Wanna do something neat?" [of my autobiography] section

75

to raucous laughter. I think he was laughing, too. About a quarter of the guests were attorneys and I haven't heard from any of them on his behalf, so it seems my meager royalties are safe for now.

Blasingame: Are there advantages to growing up in a small town and, if so, what are some of them?

Crutcher: Well, you have a huge extended family, so in general it feels safer. When I was growing up there wasn't a locked door in my entire neighborhood. The three backyards of ours and our neighbors on either side made one large hide-and-seek/kick-the-can playground. People who would have disappeared in larger cities were taken care of—given odd jobs, or handouts, or places to live. In larger cities they would have been homeless. It's hard to let a person freeze or go hungry when you know his or her name. And if you had rough or uncompromising (or deceased) parents, you could find people to take up some of that slack. There is a tribal quality.

Blasingame: Are there disadvantages to growing up in a small town and, if so, what are some of them?

Crutcher: I think every small-town inhabitant complains that everyone knows his or her business—once embarrassed, always embarrassed. And there is a certain lack of worldliness, for want of a better term. For me it translates into a less "allowing" atmosphere that is much less forgiving of behavior that falls outside the norm. Nobody cut classes when I was in school. If some downtown merchant saw a kid on the street between the hours of 8:30 AM. and 3:00 PM, he made two phone calls: one to the kid's parents and one to the school. So I guess I'd say the edges are pretty close together in a small town. I think I found my identity more easily there, but I had to get away to celebrate it.

Blasingame: *King of the Mild Frontier* is often hilarious. It's also humor that could be called self-deprecating; you seem to make fun of yourself rather than other people most of the time. Do you prefer that kind of humor? Can you explain?

Crutcher: I do prefer that kind of humor, because I know what a sharp edge making fun of other people can take on. I live for humor. Without it, I would not be a therapist and I would not be a writer. There are few things that, when applied correctly, are more healing. There is a certain meanness to making fun of others, unless you are intimately acquainted with them and have earned "fun-making permission." The more you know about a subject or a person, the deeper the humor can run, and I know myself better than anyone or anything else, so I can practice my best forms of humor on myself. Also the best humor is ironic, and my entire life is nothing if not that. I also use it to highlight what little wisdom I possess.

Blasingame: You recount your efforts as a very young man to deal with the idea of death. It was difficult, and you handled it without help, but you seem to have come to terms with the idea. In your experience as a counselor, do you find that dealing with death is a common issue for everyone? Is it common for kids?

Crutcher: The common issue is loss, and death is the trump card of loss. In the preface to one of the short stories in *Athletic Shorts* (1991, Green-willow), I said there is a case to be made that from the time of birth, when we lose a warm, enclosed, safe place to be, our lives are made up of a series of losses and our grace can be mea-sured by how we face those losses, and how we replace what is lost. What I'm talking about there is the process of grief, which is one of the most important things we do as humans—taking the risk of losing one thing so we can go on to the next. I believe our culture doesn't understand that very well, and it often tries to force us to hold on to old perceptions and beliefs that have little or no further use and that keep us stuck and afraid. If we do learn to face death, accommodate and accept it, there are few lesser changes that can tip us over, though there are certainly "fates worse than death." So, yeah, I think it's common for kids, at their developmental level, and it is common for us at ours.

Blasingame: Like the characters in your books, the people from your real life are not romanticized; they can have bad breath, acne, and total egomania. Do you enjoy capturing true-to-life human qualities and, if so, how do you go about doing it?

Crutcher: Man, I have a ringside seat for watching true-to-life qualities, starting with my own successes and failures and ending with the infinite stories (if you can "end" with something infinite) I've heard as a counselor and a questionable educator. I am fascinated by human response. My own responses to the world have allowed me to soar and [have] brought me crashing to the ground. I go about capturing all that by simply paying attention and applying my sense of humor to all I see.

Blasingame: There seems to be a huge gap between the "coonskin-cap-wearing, pimply-faced, 123-pound offensive lineman" and the tall, handsome, former college athlete with several best-selling books and a career helping dysfunctional families whom we see at young adult literature conferences. Will you fill in the gap and continue your autobiography through the college and early teaching, coaching, and counseling years at some point?

Crutcher: I think I might. I had way more fun writing this book than I deserved. The gap isn't as huge as it might seem, however. I've been afraid all my life. When I think of my preadolescence, I think of that eleven or twelve year old boy staring at the picture of the dead kid in [The Saturday Evening] *Post* magazine (readers will have to read the book to appreciate the circumstance), paralyzed at the thought of what might have happened to him and at the thought of being gone, and I'm ashamed that I couldn't get a handle on it. I have always been terrified of being a disappointment, of never being enough—as a human, as an athlete, as a lover, as a friend, as an example. I regularly give myself reasons to keep right on being terrified. But what I'm describing here is simply the business of being human. I'm afraid of the same things everyone else is afraid of; my circumstance is in no way special. As one of my greatest mentors once reminded me, Planet Earth is a tough town. If I've given myself one thing over the years that's helped, it's the capacity to not be so afraid to be afraid. The coonskin-cap-wearing, pimply-faced, 123-pound offensive lineman lives within me.

Timeline

1946 Christopher C. Crutcher is born on July 17, in Dayton, Ohio. Six weeks later, the Crutchers move to Cascade, Idaho.

1964 Crutcher graduates from Cascade High School and enrolls at Eastern Washington State College in Cheney, Washington.

1968 Crutcher graduates from Eastern with a bachelor's degree in sociology-psychology and drives to Texas where he works in construction.

1969 Crutcher returns to Eastern Washington State College where he earns a teaching certificate.

1970 Crutcher works as a maintenance man at an Oregon ski resort.

1971 In Kennewick, Washington, Crutcher teaches students who dropped out or were kicked out of public high school.

1973 Crutcher teaches high school social studies in Kennewick.

1974 Crutcher moves to California and gets a job teaching at Lakeside Elementary School in Oakland.

1975 Crutcher becomes director of Lakeside Elementary School.

1980 After quitting Lakeside, Crutcher lives on savings while writing *Running Loose*.

1982 Crutcher moves to Spokane, Washington, where he coordinates the Child Protection Team.

1983 Crutcher works as a child and family therapist at the Spokane Community Mental Health Center. *Running Loose* is published.

1986 *Stotan!* is published.

1987 *The Crazy Horse Electric Game* is published.

1991 *Athletic Shorts: Six Short Stories* is published.

1992 *The Deep End* is published.

1993 *Staying Fat for Sarah Byrnes* is published.

1994 *Ironman* is published. Crutcher wins the ALAN award for "significant contributions" to young adult literature.

1996 The film *Angus* is released. This movie was adapted from Crutcher's short story "A Brief Moment in the Life of Angus Bethune."

1998 Crutcher receives the National Intellectual Freedom Award for his ongoing efforts against censorship.

2000 Crutcher wins the distinguished Margaret A. Edwards Award for the body of his work.

2001 *Whale Talk* is published.

2003 Crutcher's autobiography, *King of the Mild Frontier,* is published.

Selected Reviews from *School Library Journal*

Ironman

April 1995

Gr 9 Up—Bo Brewster, a high school senior, is forced to attend anger-management classes after a series of run-ins with his English teacher/ex-football coach. Since those in the class are considered "felons" by outsiders, he figures the best he can hope to do is survive. The group's teacher, Mr. Nak, a Japanese American from Texas, deftly draws Bo into participating in the class, allowing him to learn plenty about himself and the running war that he has waged with his father for years. Bo spends most of his time outside of school training rigorously in preparation for a grueling triathlon. An added twist finds Bo's father providing his arch rival with an expensive bike, hoping Bo will lose and learn a lesson. The story is presented in both a third-person account of events, and through Bo's eyes in letters he writes to talk-show host Larry King, the only adult he believes will listen. Through Crutcher's masterful character development, readers will believe in Bo, empathize with the other members of the anger-management group, absorb the wisdom of Mr. Nak, and despise, yet at times pity, the boy's father. This is not a light read, as many serious issues surface, though the author's trademark dark humor (and colorful use of street language) is abundant. Crutcher has consistently penned exceptional reads for YAs, and *Ironman* is one of his strongest works yet.

King of the Mild Frontier: An Ill-Advised Autobiography

April 2003

Gr 8 Up—For those who want to know the real poop behind this popular author's characters (and, to some extent, his character), this is the book you've been waiting for. The cover photo tells it all: a white picket fence in the background, for all the world as straight and orderly and stereotyp-ically 1950s proper as the author's maddeningly rational father, "Crutch," wanted things to appear. But looming in the foreground is toothy, smiling

Chris, the short-fused emotional time bomb who regularly exploded into anger and tears. Protective of his alcoholic mom and at almost constant odds with his strict and demanding dad, Crutcher describes incidents and telling episodes from his formative years. His signature wit was sharpened in response to both his feelings of inadequacy and his competitive nature, honed by participation in high school and college sports. He addresses issues about his use of profanity in his writing for teens. Tough and tender reminiscences focus primarily on family, social, and school conflicts, but lessons derived from his career as a teacher, therapist, and writer are also described. Hyperbole lightens the mood as the author portrays himself as a young crybaby, academic misfit, and athletic klutz, utterly without self-aggrandizement. Abrupt transitions, some convoluted sentences, and non-linear progression may challenge some readers, but the narrative holds undeniable appeal for the author's fans and demonstrates the power of writing to help both reader and writer heal emotional/psychic wounds.

Stotan!
March 1986

Gr 9 Up.—A fine coming-of-age novel. Walker Dupree, the captain of Frost (Spokane, Wash.)

High School's swim team, chronicles the senior year of the tight fraternity of young men who make up the team. Lionel, orphaned at fourteen, faces a sometimes hostile world alone; Nortie lives with an abusive father whom he loves but can never please; Jeff, a brash youth with everything to live for is terminally ill. Swim coach Max Il Song tests these four young men unmercifully during Stotan Week, but he gives them a reservoir of strength they more than need before their season is over. The boys are typical of many teenagers; they think a lot about sex; their language isn't always clean. They face difficult, adult situations, violence, racial prejudice, Jeff's impending death. Crutcher's novel more than moves and entertains; it teaches. It teaches young people about responsibility, about courage and heroism, and ultimately about life itself. *Stotan!* is very, very, good.

Whale Talk

2001

Gr 8 Up—T. J. Jones, the mixed-race, larger-than-life, heroic, first-person narrator of this novel, lays out the events of his senior year, with many digressions along the way. The central plot involves T. J.'s efforts to put together a swim team of misfits, as he tries to upset the balance of power at his central Washington high school, where jocks and the narrow-minded rule. However, a number of sub-plots deal with racism, child abuse, and the efforts of the protagonist's adopted father to come to grips with a terrible mistake in his past. Crutcher uses a broad brush in an undeniably robust and energetic story that is also somewhat messy and over the top in places. T. J. himself is witty, self-assured, fearless, intelligent, and wise beyond his years. In fact, he has all of these qualities in such abundance that he's not an entirely plausible character. The novel's ending sweeps to a crescendo of emotions, as T. J.'s mentally tortured father saves a life and atones for past sins by diving in front of a bullet and dying in his son's arms. Young adults with a taste for melodrama will undeniably enjoy this effort. More discerning readers will have to look harder for the lovely passages and truths that aren't delivered with a hammer.

List of Selected Works

Athletic Shorts: Six Short Stories. New York: Greenwillow, 1991.

Chinese Handcuffs. New York: Greenwillow, 1989.

The Crazy Horse Electric Game. New York: Greenwillow, 1987.

Ironman. New York: Greenwillow, 1995.

King of the Mild Frontier. New York: Greenwillow, 2003.

Running Loose. New York: Greenwillow, 1983.

Staying Fat for Sarah Byrnes. New York: Greenwillow, 1993.

Stotan! New York: Greenwillow, 1986.

Whale Talk. New York: Greenwillow, 2001.

List of Selected Awards

ALAN Award for Significant Contribution to Adolescent Literature (1993)
American Library Association, Best Books for Young Adult Readers (1992)
Margaret A. Edwards Award (2000)
School Library Journal, Best of the Best in Young Adult Literature (1992)

Chinese Handcuffs (1989)
American Library Association, Best Books for Young Adult Readers (1989)

Crazy Horse Electric Game (1987)
American Library Association, Best Books for Young Adult Readers (1988)

School Library Journal, Best of the Best in
  Young Adult Literature (1988)

***Ironman* (1995)**
American Library Association, Best Books for
  Young Adult Readers (1996)
American Library Association, Quick Picks for
  Reluctant Young Adult Readers (1996)
School Library Journal, Best Book of the
  Year (1995)

***King of the Mild Frontier* (2003)**
American Library Association, Best Books for
  Young Adult Readers (2004)

***Running Loose* (1983)**
American Library Association, Best Books for
  Young Adult Readers (1983)
School Library Journal, Best of the Best in
  Young Adult Literature (2000)

***Staying Fat for Sarah Byrnes* (1993)**
American Library Association, Best Books for
  Young Adults (1994)
School Library Journal, Best Book of the
  Year (1993)

Stotan! (1986)

American Library Association, Best Books for
Young Adult Readers (1986)
School Library Journal, Best of the Best in
Young Adult Literature (1986)

Whale Talk (2001)

American Library Association, Best Books for
Young Adults (2002)

Glossary

ALA American Library Association, the oldest and largest association of libraries in the world whose job is to create quality libraries and information services across the United States.

ALAN award Prestigious lifetime award given every year for outstanding contributions to the field of children's literature by the Assembly on Literature for Adolescents of NCTE (National Council of Teachers of English).

anticipated Expected.

ban To prohibit or outlaw.

banter Teasing, playful comments.

blasphemous Speech that disrespects religious beliefs or ideas.

camaraderie Companionship.

censor To prohibit or repress something that is considered negative or damaging.

chaotic Confused, or lacking order.

conservative People (or beliefs) who are traditional or cautious of change.

contrived Something that is obviously planned or that doesn't seem natural.

disdain Rejection of a person or thing that seems inferior.

Episcopalian A member of the Episcopalian Protestant Church.

fundamentalist A strong believer in a set of strict traditional (usually religious) values, often while rejecting other beliefs.

ghastly Horrible.

grapple To struggle or deal with.

grueling Tough, difficult.

jibes Sharp remarks that poke fun at someone or something.

jurisdiction Authority or control over a certain territory.

loutish Crude, loud, rude, ill-mannered.

Margaret A. Edwards Award Distinguished award given every year to a YA author for his or her entire body of work by the Young Adult Library Services Association.

Oral Roberts A famous American Christian preacher and televangelist.

pining Longing, yearning after.

protagonist A main character.

provocative Disturbing, challenging, or stimulating.

psychology The study of mental behavior.

rational Logical, levelheaded, sane.

sociology The study of human society and its institutions and organizations.

Spartans Ancient Greek citizens from the city of Sparta known for their bravery and rigid self-discipline.

spontaneous Natural, impulsive, without thought.

stamina Strength (physical or mental) to resist tiredness or difficulty.

staunch Firm.

stoic A person who calmly accepts all suffering and difficulties.

taboos Prohibitions imposed by society.

tentative Unsure, indecisive.

testosterone A hormone in the body responsible for male characteristics.

thesaurus A book of words and their synonyms.

whim A sudden impulse.

For More Information

Due to the changing nature of Internet links, the Rosen Publishing Group, Inc., has developed an online list of Web sites related to the subject of this book. This site is updated regularly. Please use this link to access the list:

http://www.rosenlinks.com/lab/chcr

For Further Reading

Crutcher, Chris. *King of the Mild Frontier*. New York: Greenwillow, 2003.

Davis, Terry. *Presenting Chris Crutcher*. New York: Twayne Publishers, 1997.

Frederick, Heather Vogel. "Chris Crutcher: 'What's Known Can't Be Unknown'" (interview), *Publishers Weekly*, February 20, 1995, pp. 183–184.

Jenkinson, Dave. "Portraits: Chris Crutcher: YA Author Bats 4 for 4 on ALA's 'Best Books for Young Adults' Lists." *Emergency Librarian*, Jan./Feb. 1991., pp. 67–72.

Bibliography

Atkins, Holly. An Interview with Chris
    Crutcher. The *St. Petersburg Times*
    Online. "We're Talking Books Here."
    October 20, 2003. Retrieved January
    2004 (http://www.sptimes.com/
    2003/10/20/Nie/An_interview_with_
    Chr.shtml).

Bush, Margaret A. Review of *Chinese Hand-
    cuffs*. The *Horn Book Magazine*,
    July-August 1989. p. 487.

Carmel Clay Public Library Young Adult.
    Author Feature: Chris Crutcher. Retrieved
    December 2003 (http://www.carmel.lib.
    in.us/ya/crutcher.htm).

Carter, Betty. Interview with Chris Crutcher.
    "Eyes Wide Open." *School Library Journal*

Online. June 1, 2000. Retrieved December 2003 (http://www.schoollibraryjournal.com/index.asp?layout=articleArchive&articleid=CA153044).

Chelton, Mary K. Review of *Running Loose*. *Voice of Youth Advocates*, Vol. 6, No. 1, April 1983, p. 36.

Chris Crutcher's Authorized Web Site. Retrieved December 2003 (http://www.chriscrutcher.com).

Crutcher, Chris. *Athletic Shorts: Six Short Stories*. New York: Harper Tempest, 2002.

Crutcher, Chris. *Chinese Handcuffs*. New York: Laurel Leaf Books, 1989.

Crutcher, Chris. *The Crazy Horse Electric Game*. New York: Laurel Leaf Books, 1987.

Crutcher, Chris. *King of the Mild Frontier*. New York: Greenwillow Books, 2003.

Crutcher, Chris. *Running Loose*. New York: Laurel Leaf Books, 1986.

Crutcher, Chris. *Staying Fat for Sarah Byrnes*. New York: Harper Tempest, 2003.

Crutcher, Chris. *Stotan!* New York: Harper Tempest, 2003.

Crutcher, Chris. *Whale Talk*. New York: Greenwillow Books, 2001.

Davis, Terry. *Presenting Chris Crutcher*. New York: Twayne Publishers, 1997.

Greenway, Betty. "Chris Crutcher—Hero or Villain? Responses of Parents, Students, Critics, Teachers," ALAN Review, Vol. 22, No. 1, Fall 1994. ALAN Home Page. Retrieved January 2004 (http://scholar.lib.vt.edu/ejournals/ALAN/fall94/Greenway.html).

Hedblad, Alan, ed. *Something About the Author*, Vol. 99. Detroit: Gale Group, 1999.

Jones, Trev. Review of *Running Loose. School Library Journal*, Vol. 29, No. 9, May 1983, p. 80.

K-I-D REACH—The Online Reading Center. "Chris Crutcher." Retrieved December 2003 (http://www.westga.edu/~kidreach/ChrisCrutcher.html).

McDonnell, Christine. "New Voices, New Visions: Chris Crutcher." The *Horn Book Magazine*, Vol. LXIV, May-June 1988, pp. 332–335.

Morning, Todd. Review of *The Crazy Horse Electric Game*. The *Horn Book Magazine*, Vol. LXIII, No. 6, November-December 1987, p. 741.

Random House Children's Books. Authors/Illustrators: Chris Crutcher. Retrieved December 2003 (http://www.randomhouse.com/teachers/authors/crut.html).

Senick, Gerard J., ed. *Children's Literature Review*, Vol. 28, 1992, pp. 98–108.

Sheffer, Susannah. "An Adult Reads Chris Crutcher." *The ALAN Review*, Volume 24, Number 3, pp. 10–11, 1997 (http://scholar.lib.vt.edu/ejournals/ALAN/spring97/s97-10Sheffer.html).

Silvey, Anita. Review of *The Crazy Horse Electric Game*, The *Horn Book Magazine*, Vol, LXIII, No. 6, November-December 1987, p. 1966.

Smith, Louisa. "Limitations on Young Adult Fiction: An Interview with Chris Crutcher." *The Lion and the Unicorn*, June 1992, pp. 66–73.

Sutherland, Zena. Review of *Running Loose*. *Bulletin of the Center for Children's Books*, Vol. 36, No. 9, May 1983, p. 165.

TeenReads.com. Author Profile: Chris Crutcher. Retrieved December 2003 (http://www.teenreads.com/authors/au-crutcher-chris-2.asp).

Vasilakis, Nancy. Review of *Athletic Shorts*. The *Horn Book Magazine*, September-October 1991, pp. 602–603.

Zvirin, Stephanie. "The YA Connection: *Chinese Handcuffs*." *Booklist*, August 1989, p. 1966.

Source Notes

Introduction

1. Chris Crutcher, *King of the Mild Frontier* (New York: Greenwillow Books, 2003), p. 256.
2. Chris Crutcher, foreword to *Athletic Shorts: Six Short Stories* (New York: Harper Tempest, 2002), p. xi.

Chapter 1

1. Chris Crutcher, telephone interview with Thomas Kowikowski for *Authors and Artists for Young Adults*, March 11, 1992, pp. 85–95. Cited in *Something About the Author*, p. 60.
2. Chris Crutcher, *Running Loose* (New York: Laurel Leaf Books, 1986), p. 26.
3. Crutcher, *King of the Mild Frontier* (New York: Greenwillow Books, 2003), p. 20.
4. Ibid., p. 2.

Chapter 2

1. Alan Hedblad, ed., *Something About the Author*, Vol. 99 (Detroit: Gale Group, 1999), p. 61.
2. Chris Crutcher, *Staying Fat for Sarah Byrnes* (New York: Harper Tempest, 2003), p. 85.
3. Crutcher, *King of the Mild Frontier* (New York: Greenwillow Books, 2003), p. 6.
4. Ibid., p. 127.
5. Ibid., p. 133.
6. Terry Davis, *Presenting Chris Crutcher* (New York: Twayne Publishers, 1997), p. 21.
7. Ibid., pp. 21–22.

CHAPTER 3

1. Chris Crutcher, *King of the Mild Frontier* (New York: Greenwillow Books, 2003), p. 49.
2. Ibid.
3. Ibid., p. 51.
4. Chris Crutcher, *Running Loose* (New York: Laurel Leaf Books, 1986), p. 15.
5. Alan Hedblad, ed., *Something About the Author*, Vol. 99 (Detroit: Gale Group, 1999), p. 61.
6. Crutcher, *King of the Mild Frontier*, (New York: Greenwillow Books, 2003), p. 63.
7. Chris Crutcher. *Chinese Handcuffs* (New York: Laurel Leaf Books, 1989), p. 18.

CHAPTER 4

1. Chris Crutcher, *The Crazy Horse Electric Game* (New York: Laurel Leaf Books, 1987), p. 124.

CHAPTER 5

1. Chris Crutcher, interview with Dave Jenkinson. "Portraits: Chris Crutcher," *Emergency Librarian*, Vol. 18, No. 3, January-February 1991, pp. 66–71. Cited in *Children's Literature Review*, Vol. 28, p. 99.
2. Alan Hedblad, ed., *Something About the Author*, Vol. 99 (Detroit: Gale Group, 1999), p. 62.
3. Louisa Smith. "Limitations on Young Adult Fiction: An Interview with Chris Crutcher." *The Lion and the Unicorn*, June 1992, p. 67.
4. Terry Davis, *Presenting Chris Crutcher* (New York: Greenwillow Books, 2003), pp. 80–81.
5. Chris Crutcher, *The Crazy Horse Electric Game* (New York: Laurel Leaf Books, 1987), p. 73.
6. Margaret A. Bush, review of *Chinese Handcuffs*, The *Horn Book Magazine*, July-August 1989, p. 487.
7. Stephanie Zvirin, "The YA Connection: *Chinese Handcuffs*," *Booklist*, August 1989, p. 1966.
8. Review of *Chinese Handcuffs*, *Kirkus Reviews*, February 15, 1989, p. 290.
9. Smith, p. 72.
10. Ibid., p. 71.

CHAPTER 6

1. Alan Hedblad, ed., *Something About the Author*, Vol. 99 (Detroit: Gale Group, 1999), p. 62.
2. Chris Crutcher, *Running Loose* (New York: Laurel Leaf Books, 1986), p. 15.

3. Mary K. Chelton, review of *Running Loose*, V*oice of Youth Advocates*, Vol. 6, No. 1, April 1983, p. 36.

4. Zena Sutherland, review of *Running Loose*, *Bulletin of the Center for Children's Books*, Vol. 36, No. 9, May 1983, p. 165.

5. Trev Jones, review of *Running Loose*, *School Library Journal*, Vol. 29, No. 9, May 1983, p. 80.

6. Crutcher, *King of the Mild Frontier* (New York: Greenwillow Books, 2003), pp. 225–226.

7. Cited on Carmel Clay Public Library Web Site. Young Adult. "Featured Author—Chris Crutcher." Retrieved December 2003 (http://www.carmel.lib.in.us/ya/crutcher.htm)

8. Chris Crutcher, interview with Betty Carter, "Eyes Wide Open," *School Library Journal* Online, published June 1, 2000, retrieved December 2003 (http://www.schoollibraryjournal. com/index.asp?layout=articleArchive& articleid=CA153044)

9. Anita Silvey, review of *The Crazy Horse Electric Game*, The *Horn Book Magazine*, Vol, LXIII, N. 6, November-December 1987, p. 741.

10. Nancy Vasilakis, review of *Athletic Shorts*, The *Horn Book Magazine*, September-October 1991, p. 603.

11. Louisa Smith, "Limitations on Young Adult Fiction: An Interview with Chris Crutcher," *The Lion and the Unicorn*, June 1992, p. 69.

12. Chris Crutcher, interview with Betty Carter.

13. Holly Atkins, interview with Chris Crutcher, The St. Petersburg Times Online, "We're Talking Books Here," published October 20, 2003, retrieved January 2004 (http://www.sptimes.com/2003/10/20/Nie/An_interview_with_Chr.shtml)

Index

About the Author

Michael A. Sommers is a freelance writer with a degree in literature.

Photo Credits

Cover, p. 2 courtesy of Chris Crutcher.

Series Designer: Tahara Anderson; **Editor:** Annie Sommers; **Photo Researcher:** Hillary Arnold